MUSIC+LYRICS BY
RYAN SCOTT OLIVER
VOLUME 1

CONTENTS

*Music by Eric Day
Proof Editors: Brett Ryback, Kat Sherrell
Photographs: Matthew Murphy

RYAN SCOTT OLIVER wrote the music and lyrics for *35mm*, *Darling* (as seen on the 10th season of NBC's *The Apprentice*), and *Mrs. Sharp* (2008 Richard Rodgers Award Winner, workshop at Playwrights Horizons starring Jane Krakowski, directed by Michael Greif). His work has been presented at the Kennedy Center, Joe's Pub, and the New York Musical Theatre Festival, and has also been heard Off-Broadway in *We the People* (TheatreWorksUSA), on the YouTube webseries *The Battery's Down* ("This is Your Life," et al; CD available through Sh-K-Boom Records), as well as in cabarets and showcases around the world. He is the recipient of a 2008 Jonathan Larson Grant, the 2007 Harold Adamson Award for Excellence in Lyric Writing (ASCAP), and a 2007 Dramatists Guild Fellowship. He is represented by Jessica Amato at the Gersh Agency.

THE BALLAD OF SARA BERRY

from *35mm*

Music and Lyrics by
RYAN SCOTT OLIVER

www.ryanscottoliver.com

4

Harmonize all voices similarly when only one staff is present, keeping the men in the middle and high registers, and the women in the low and middle (belt range).

10

"The Ballad of Sara Berry" - 8

www.ryanscottoliver.com

www.ryanscottoliver.com

12

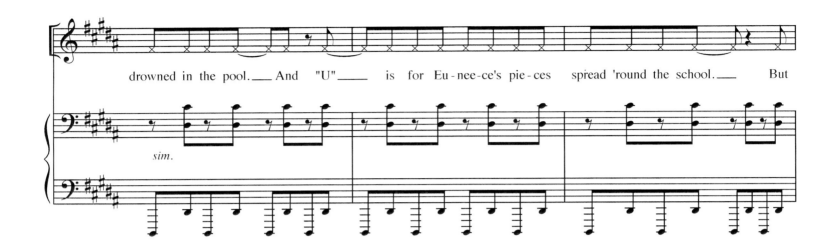

drowned in the pool.___ And "U"___ is for Eu-nee-ce's pie-ces spread 'round the school.___ But

sim.

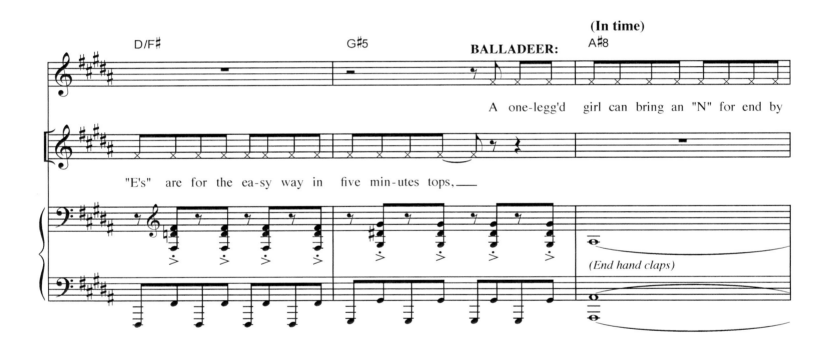

A one-legg'd girl can bring an "N" for end by

"E's" are for the ea-sy way in five min-utes tops,___

(End hand claps)

call-ing the cops.___ You got your sil-ver, Sa-ra! You got your crown,___ You got their

www.ryanscottoliver.com

THE SERAPH

from *35mm*

Music and Lyrics by
RYAN SCOTT OLIVER

*This figure is not an improvisation.

"The Seraph" - 1

www.ryanscottoliver.com

feel him___ rest his Se - raph head,_____ warm, a - gainst my chest,___ Don't know

why it should be,___ but by___ the An - gel,_____ I am___

___ bless'd._____ I

Freely

don't be - lieve___ in God.___ I think Je - sus was just a man.___ But

26

ON MONDAY

from *35mm*

Music and Lyrics by
RYAN SCOTT OLIVER

www.ryanscottoliver.com

CARALEE

from *35mm*

Music and Lyrics by
RYAN SCOTT OLIVER

"Caralee" - 1

www.ryanscottoliver.com

42

LOST BOY

from *Darling*

Music and Lyrics by
RYAN SCOTT OLIVER

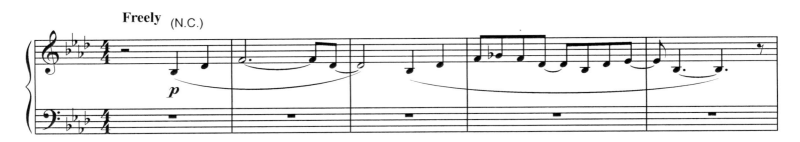

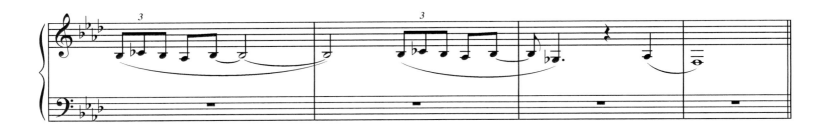

www.ryanscottoliver.com

WHEN LILY CAME

from *Darling*

Music and Lyrics by
RYAN SCOTT OLIVER

"When Lily Came" - 1

www.ryanscottoliver.com

54

"When Lily Came" - 2

www.ryanscottoliver.com

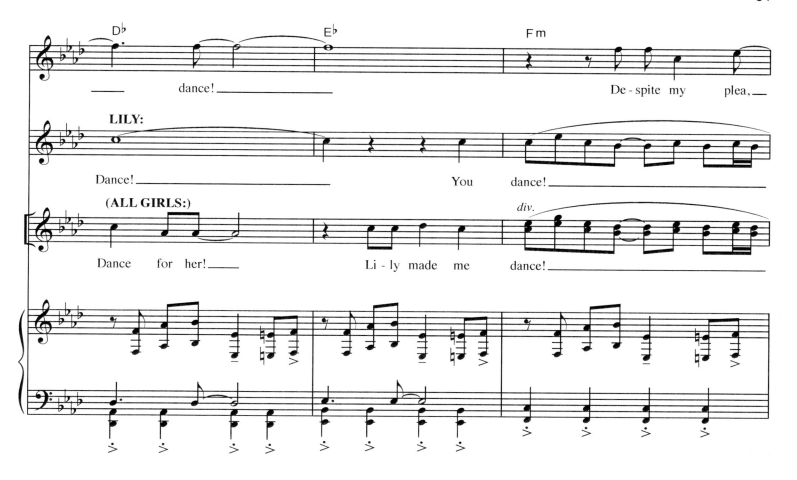

DULL LITTLE ACHE

from *Darling*

Music and Lyrics by
RYAN SCOTT OLIVER

64

68

"Dull Little Ache" - 6

www.ryanscottoliver.com

THE VIEW FROM HERE

from *Darling*

Music and Lyrics by
RYAN SCOTT OLIVER

Music and Lyrics © 2007 by Ryan Scott Oliver. © 2011 ARESSO MUSIC PUBLISHING.
All rights reserved.

www.ryanscottoliver.com

74

76

"The View from Here" - 4 www.ryanscottoliver.com

78

A HYPOCHONDRIAC'S SONG

from *Out of My Head*

Music and Lyrics by
RYAN SCOTT OLIVER

www.ryanscottoliver.com

82

"A Hypochondriac's Song" - 3

www.ryanscottoliver.com

84

CRAYON GIRL

from *Out of My Head*

Music and Lyrics by
RYAN SCOTT OLIVER

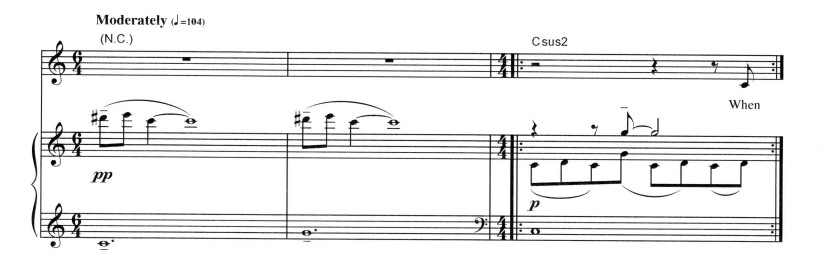

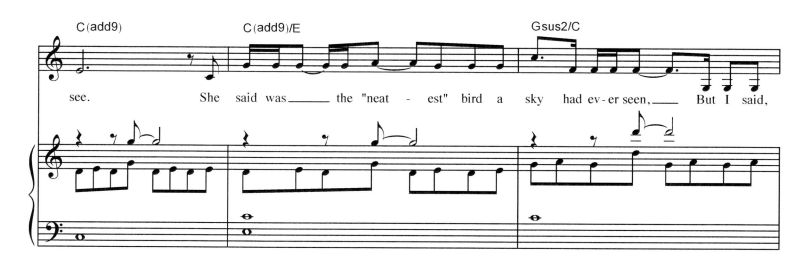

WHAT IT'S WORTH

from *Out of My Head*

Music and Lyrics by
RYAN SCOTT OLIVER

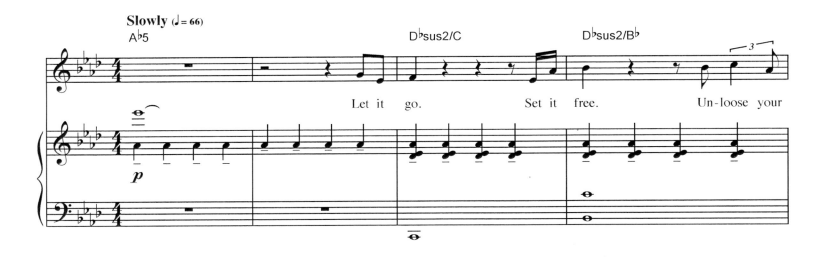

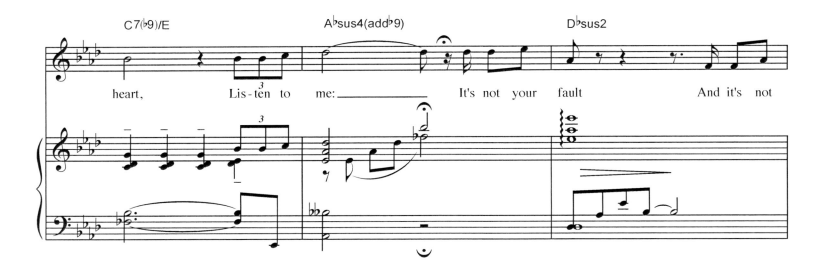

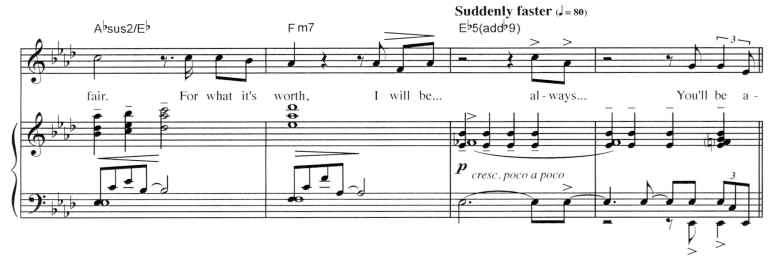

www.ryanscottoliver.com

SARAH FITCHNER

from *Out of My Head*

Music and Lyrics by
RYAN SCOTT OLIVER

Lyrics: Se-venth grade,___ Mrs.___ Bram-mer's___ class: I have no friends. Though my class-mates give me ma-ny names: "Smel-ly Sa-rah," "Fug-ly Fitch-ner," "Sa-rah Mc-Ass-

www.ryanscottoliver.com

108

"Sarah Fitchner" - 5

www.ryanscottoliver.com

110

www.ryanscottoliver.com

112

HALFWAY

Music and Lyrics by
RYAN SCOTT OLIVER

Music and Lyrics © 2008 by Ryan Scott Oliver. © 2011 ARESSO MUSIC PUBLISHING.

www.ryanscottoliver.com

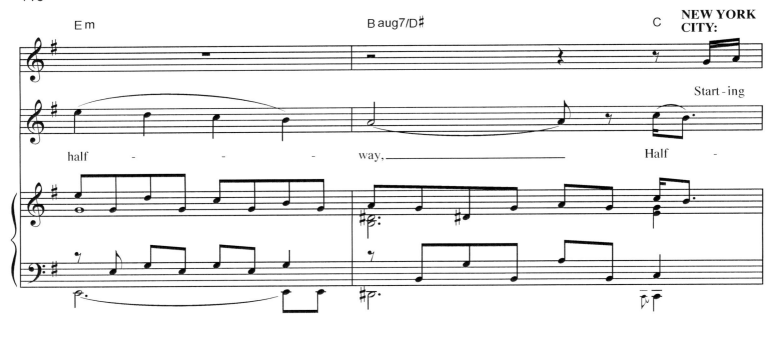

NEW YORK CITY:

Start-ing half - - - - way,_____ Half -

south on Se-venth_ Ave.,_ Go_ the Hol - land Tun-nel_ way._ And de-

-way...

-pend-ing how much traf-fic ya have,_ Ten_ to for-ty mi-nutes from N. Y. to N. J._ Meet you

118

"Halfway" - 4

124

for Cait Doyle's Hot Mess in Manhattan
THE MESS

Music and Lyrics by
RYAN SCOTT OLIVER

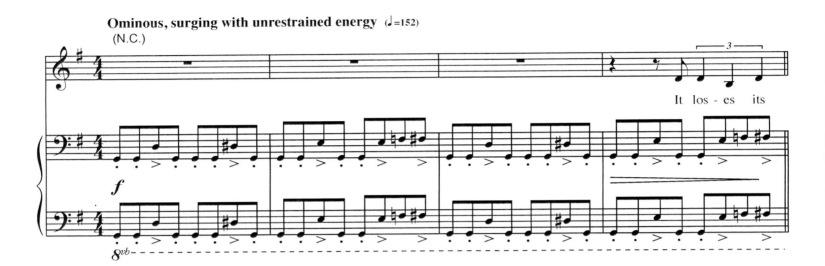

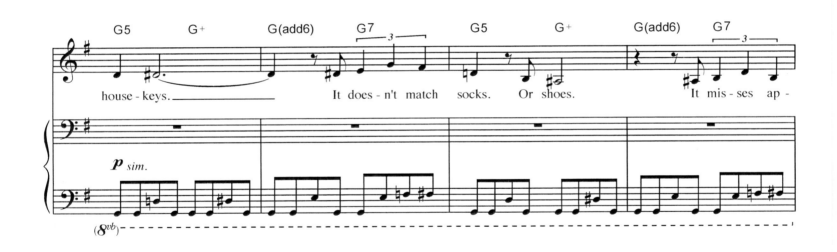

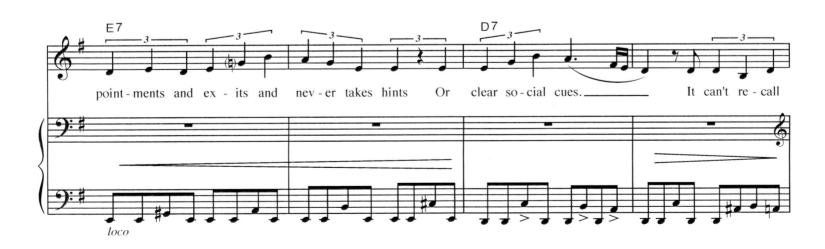

www.ryanscottoliver.com

128

129

132

134

THE PLANE
(IS GOING DOWN)

Music by ERIC DAY
Lyrics by RYAN SCOTT OLIVER

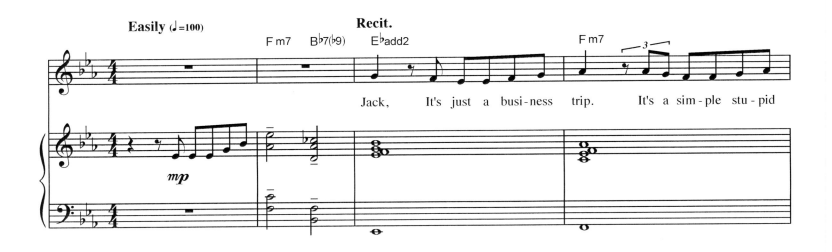

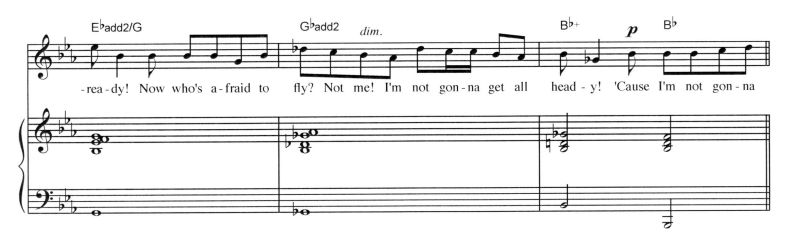

www.ryanscottoliver.com

ANOTHER VOICE:
Attention passengers, this is your captain speaking. Sorry for the delay; we now have permission for departure. Flight crew, prepare for take-off.

Mom - my said to sim - ply search some - where in my soul, And see that I don't fear to fly, I fear to lose c... The plane is go - ing up... The plane is go - ing up... I'm gon - na die I'm gon - na die I'm gon - na die I'm gon - na die!

TO DO

Music and Lyrics by
RYAN SCOTT OLIVER

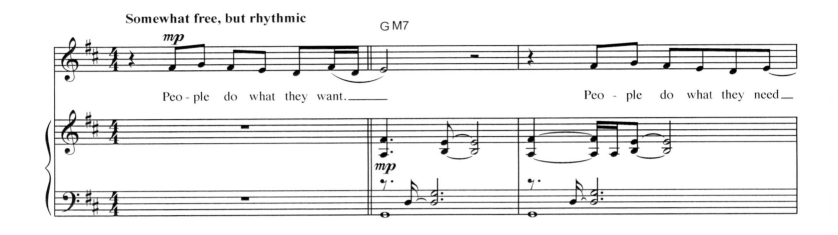

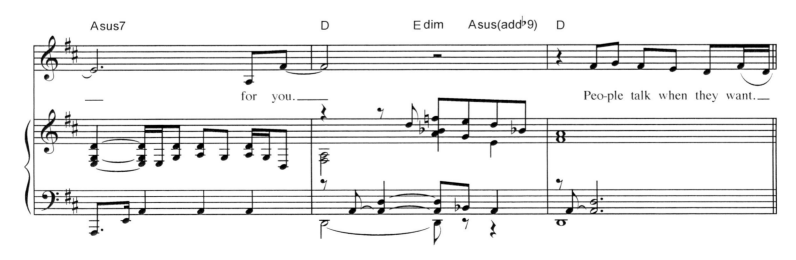

www.ryanscottoliver.com

146

ODYSSEY

Music and Lyrics by
RYAN SCOTT OLIVER

www.ryanscottoliver.com

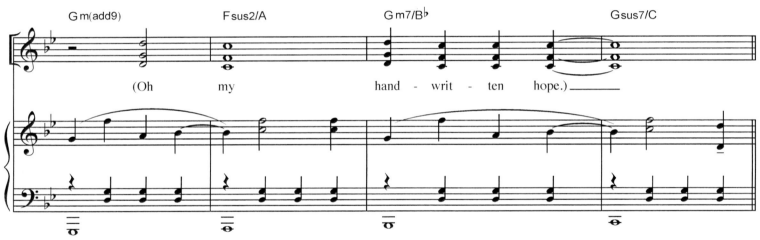

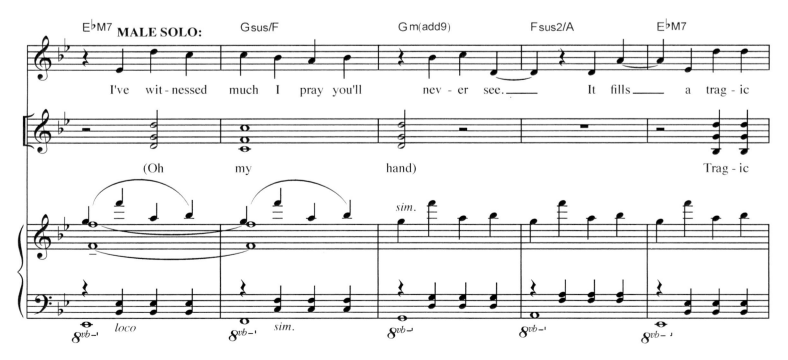

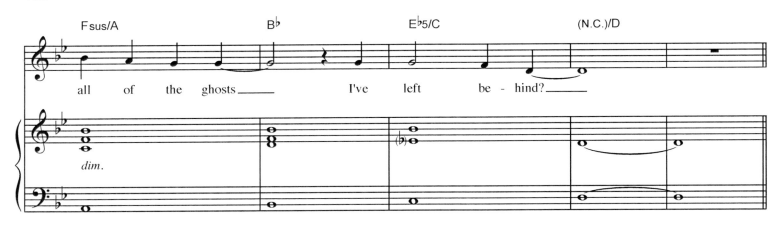

all of the ghosts _____ I've left be - hind? _____

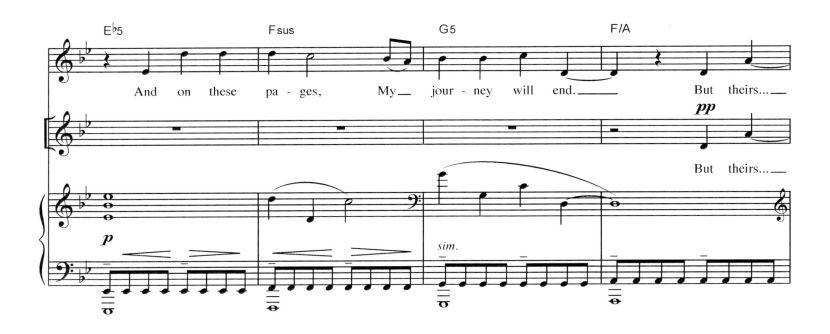

And on these pa - ges, My _ jour - ney will end. _____ But theirs... _____

pp

But theirs... _____

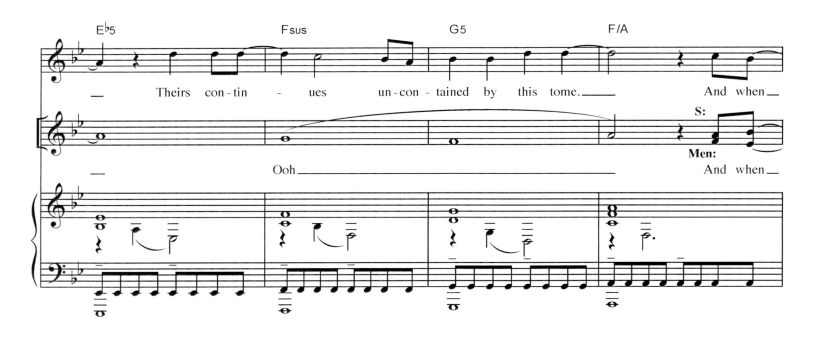

_ Theirs con - tin - ues un - con - tained by this tome. _____ And when _

S:

Ooh _____ And when _

Men:

And when _

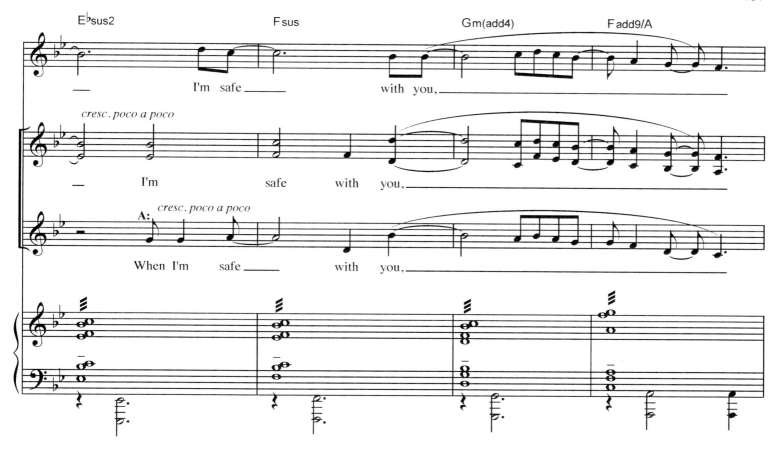

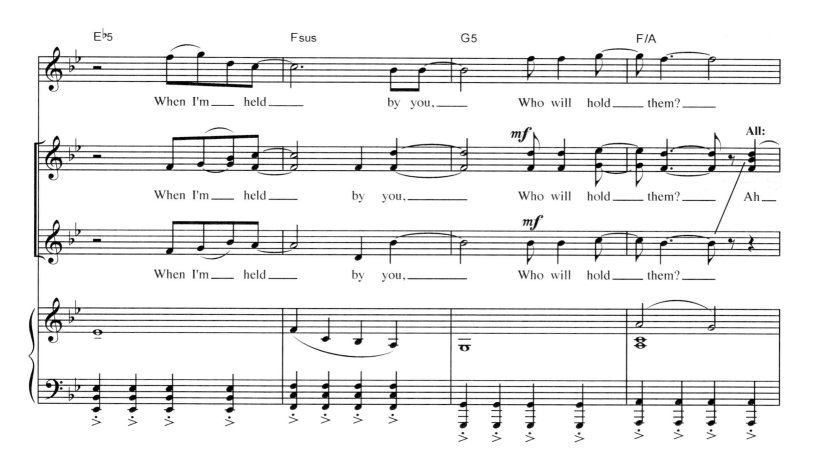

160

FEMALE SOLO:

Where the road ends, I will guide you.

Through the night-storm, I will guide you.

As blood and air are Al-ways as-tride you,

+2 Tenors:
I'm be-side you,

ALL:
+S/A:
+Men:
And I will guide you

164

"Odyssey" - 15

www.ryanscottoliver.com

MAKE ME A PICTURE OF THE SUN

Words by EMILY DICKINSON
Music by RYAN SCOTT OLIVER

www.ryanscottoliver.com

166

168

"Make Me a Picture of the Sun" - 4   www.ryanscottoliver.com

PEACE
(AN ELEGY)

Music and Lyrics by
RYAN SCOTT OLIVER

Peace. Go home my friend.

I wrote this song _____ for you. _____ It means I'm sor-ry. _____ It means that I

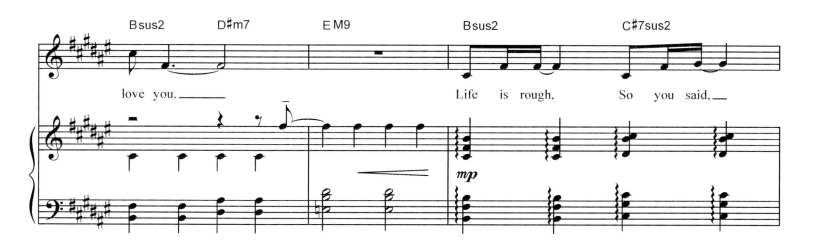

love you. _____ Life is rough, So you said, _____

STUPID BOYS

Music and Lyrics by
RYAN SCOTT OLIVER

www.ryanscottoliver.com

172

Back-up harmonies are written for two tenors, but may be performed by men, women, or both; displace the octave as necessary.

www.ryanscottoliver.com

174

ACKNOWLEDGMENTS

I owe very much to many people, but this short list offers my gratitude for the creation of this book:

Thanks to Matthew Murphy, the photographer whose work inspired *35mm* and whose passion inspires my life; to Kirsten Guenther, my longtime collaborator on *Out of My Head* and *Mrs. Sharp*; to Zina Goldrich, who gave me the idea; to Kat Sherrell for her editing; to Alex Brightman, Cait Doyle, Matt Hinkley, Jay Armstrong Johnson, Lindsay Mendez, and Will Van Dyke for their singular influence on various songs in this book; to Brett Ryback, my *Darling* collaborator who challenges and humbles me; to Jessica Amato, my agent, with whom I daily share the winnings of a long-past gamble; and to Sherry and Scott Oliver, whose unquestioning investment makes everything possible.

COMPOSER'S NOTES

So, thanks for picking up this book! A few tips you may find useful:

Nearly all of the songs contained herein were written for piano and then orchestrated, and now they have been re-written for piano based on those orchestrations. In the event you do purchase band parts for a song, you should also purchase the separate band-piano part, as those in this volume represent an entire band in two hands, and in the spirit of good orchestration the sparser part will allow other instruments to stand out. (See below for information on how to purchase band parts.)

And speaking of those orchestrations, many instrument parts are already available for purchase, and those unwritten may be custom-composed by request!

Having come from a more rigid, classical background, I do intend for the notes on the page to be played. With the exception of a few of the "poppier" songs (such as "On Monday," or "To Do"), the music is really not meant to be "faked."

Vocal improvisation may be encouraged, but use caution!

Most musical theatre people are familiar with the more established versions of the genre's classic songs, and now revisions or alterations are welcomed as bringing new life to the old (as with songs like "Somewhere Over the Rainbow," for example). But most of the songs in this book haven't yet been given their "fair shot" as intended by the composer, and because of that I encourage you to deliver what is on the page. Besides, each performance will be inherently different and special anyway… "Let it come from you, then it will be new" and all that.

And on the subject, in our new tech age, take advantage of YouTube, and pay special attention to tempo and dynamic markings. As a writer I avoid tempo *rit.*s if I can (though you'll find them in some of the older songs), and so unless I indicate them, make sure to keep the beat going steadily.

Songs like "Sarah Fitchner," "Caralee," and "The Mess" are perfect for cabaret acts in their storytelling, so feel free to embellish and add dialogue throughout to make the stories your own.

Re: "*opt.*" notes, please note that the "big notes" are the ones I suggest you take. For some vocalists the smaller notes may be just what the doctor ordered; for others they could be just a big mistake.

And it's a good time to mention that key transpositions are also available by request for every song, whether it's down a step ("The View from Here" is awfully high) or a gender-bending transposition (amazing how often girls will sing "Lost,"—er, "Boy").

To make a request for band parts, key transpositions, or to purchase other songs not contained in this book, please email us at sheetmusic@ryanscottoliver.com.

And you can always find out the latest at www.ryanscottoliver.com.

PERFORMER'S RESOURCE

Below you'll find helpful information about the songs in this book, including a general overview by genre, key, and range; the song's context or story synopsis; a recommended YouTube clip to watch the song performed; where applicable, a suggested audition cut; and a list of band parts currently available.

"The Ballad of Sara Berry" from *35MM*, based on a photograph by Matthew Murphy
    Genre: Pop, Uptempo
    Key/Range: G# minor; F#3—E5
    Context: *Pressured by her family to be crowned prom queen, Sara Berry will do anything to obtain that glorified title, including murder.*
    Watch This Performance: http://www.youtube.com/watch?v=5SJPJI6L3P8 *(performed by Lindsay Mendez, Alex Brightman, Jay Armstrong Johnson, and Natalie Weiss)*
    Suggested Audition Cut: "You got your silver, Sara! You got your crown," to the end.
    Band Parts Available: PIANO, GUITAR, BASS, DRUMS, CELLO, VIOLIN, SYNTH, more

"Caralee" from *35MM*, based on a photograph by Matthew Murphy
    Genre: Comedic, Story Song
    Key/Range: B major; D#3—F4
    Context: *A "manny" (male nanny) describes the horror of Caralee, the terror he is paid to look after.*
    Watch This Performance: http://www.youtube.com/watch?v=yH_uBzlS9-Q *(performed by Jay Armstrong Johnson)*
    Suggested Audition Cut: "Caralee likes spaghetti" to the end.
    Band Parts Available: PIANO, GUITAR, BASS, DRUMS, CELLO, VIOLIN/VIOLA, SYNTH, more

"Crayon Girl" from *OUT OF MY HEAD*, book by Kirsten Guenther
    Genre: Story Song
    Key/Range: C major; G3—E5
    Context: *As an artist struggles to translate her visions onto paper, she questions whether or not she should continue her career as an artist due to negativity from her mother.*
    Watch This Performance: http://www.youtube.com/watch?v=1WgJWudMX5A *(performed by Lindsay Mendez)*
    Suggested Audition Cut: Two bars before "In my mind there is a story" to the end.
    Band Parts Available: PIANO, BASS, DRUMS, more

"Dull Little Ache" from *DARLING*, book by B. T. Ryback
    Genre: Sexy Mid-tempo
    Key/Range: Bb major; F3—Db5
    Context: *Madame Stella explains the highs and lows of prostitution as she thinks of what one does to make a living.*
    Watch This Performance: http://www.youtube.com/watch?v=S-dZL-kytck *(performed by Lindsay Mendez, Jay Armstrong Johnson, and Alex Brightman)*
    Suggested Audition Cut: "Some want to get" (singing the boys' parts) to "Oh, all right."
    Band Parts Available: PIANO, GUITAR, BASS, DRUMS, CELLO, more

"Halfway"
    Genre: Ballad, Love Song, Gay Interest
    Key/Range: G major; LOS ANGELES: (D3 to G4), NEW YORK CITY: (D3 to A4)
    Context: *Two lovers living on opposite coasts meet each other in the middle of the country, their anticipation building as the separate road trips progress.*
    Watch This Performance: http://www.youtube.com/watch?v=AK1FEwtt3t0 *(performed by Jay Armstrong Johnson and Morgan Karr)*
    Band Parts Available: PIANO, GUITAR, BASS, DRUMS, CELLO, more

"A Hypochondriac's Song" from *OUT OF MY HEAD*, book by Kirsten Guenther
    Genre: Mid-Tempo Ballad, Story Song, Comedy Song
    Key/Range: Bb major; F3 to D#5
    Context: *Ridiculously plagued by her fear of death, a girl struggles through everyday life as she strives to find a man who will put up with her crazy phobias.*
    Watch This Performance: http://www.youtube.com/watch?v=mxFeUUEq_44 *(performed by Lizzie Klemperer)*
    Suggested Audition Cut: "Get me out of my mind!" to the end.
    Band Parts Available: PIANO, BASS, DRUMS, more

"Lost Boy" from _DARLING,_ book by B. T. Ryback
> **Genre:** Ballad, Story Song
> **Key/Range:** A♭ major; F2 to G♭4
> **Context:** _Peter chronicles hardships in his life that make him feel as if he doesn't belong._
> **Watch This Performance:** http://www.youtube.com/watch?v=HeUhDslnyDo _(performed by Alex Brightman)_
> **Suggested Audition Cut:** Two bars before "But doesn't every person deserve a second chance?" to the end.
> **Band Parts Available:** PIANO, GUITAR, BASS, DRUMS, CELLO, more

"Make Me a Picture of the Sun," words by Emily Dickinson (1830—1886)
> **Genre:** Jazz torch song
> **Key/Range:** D major; A3 to D5
> **Context:** _A setting of Emily Dickinson's classic poem._
> **Band Parts Available:** PIANO, GUITAR, BASS, DRUMS, more

"The Mess"
> **Genre:** Pop, Comedic
> **Key/Range:** G major; A♯3 to E♭5
> **Context:** _A girl explains why she is a complete mess._
> **Watch This Performance:** http://www.youtube.com/watch?v=3-U7wPxTAIE _(performed by Cait Doyle)_
> **Suggested Audition Cut:** "I do auditions" to the end.
> **Band Parts Available:** PIANO, GUITAR, BASS, DRUMS, CELLO, SYNTH, more

Odyssey
> **Genre:** Pop/Gospel Ballad with Chorus
> **Key/Range:** B♭ major; D3 to A4
> **Context:** _A soldier abandons a defeated, war-torn land, returning home to the comfort of his lover._
> **Watch This Performance:** http://www.youtube.com/watch?v=3UWk7NIEXWE _(performed by Eric Michael Krop)_
> **Suggested Audition Cut:** "I've witnessed much I pray" to "I've left behind."
> **Band Parts Available:** PIANO, GUITAR, BASS, DRUMS, CELLO, SYNTH, more

"On Monday" from _35MM,_ based on a photograph by Matthew Murphy
> **Genre:** Pop Up-tempo
> **Key/Range:** C major; G3 to E♭5
> **Context:** _A fast-moving girl learns that the greatest love takes the greatest while._
> **Watch This Performance:** http://www.youtube.com/watch?v=4BV79eSArCU _(performed by Natalie Weiss)_
> **Suggested Audition Cut:** "You are cute, but juvenile" to the end.
> **Band Parts Available:** PIANO, GUITAR, BASS, DRUMS, CELLO, SYNTH, more

Peace (A Eulogy)
> **Genre:** Ballad
> **Key/Range:** F♯ major; C♯4 to C♯5.
> **Context:** _Final words for a lost friend._
> **Band Parts Available:** PIANO, more

"The Plane (is Going Down)," Music by Eric Day
> **Genre:** Story Song, Comedic
> **Key/Range:** E♭ major; C♭3 to E♭4
> **Context:** _A man is forced to face his fear of flying when he is asked to go on a business trip._
> **Watch This Performance:** http://www.youtube.com/watch?v=2j1OUYBOmT8 _(performed by Ryan Scott Oliver)_
> **Suggested Audition Cut:** " 'A' stands for Albatross" through first chorus "see that I don't fear to fly, I fear to lose c—c—" then cut to pick-ups to the second-to-last bar, "I'm gonna die, I'm gonna die, I'm gonna die, I'm gonna die!" end.
> **Band Parts Available:** PIANO, BASS, DRUMS, more

"Sarah Fitchner" from _OUT OF MY HEAD,_ book by Kirsten Guenther
> **Genre:** Story Song
> **Key/Range:** B♭ major; G3 to F4
> **Context:** _A childhood of being ditched by her female friends prepares Sarah to stand up for a girl in the same situation._
> **Watch This Performance:** http://www.youtube.com/watch?v=P1vPWhu8fSs _(performed by Kathleen Gail Hennessey)_
> **Suggested Audition Cut:** "Then one by one I watch our friends" to the end.
> **Band Parts Available:** PIANO, DRUMS, CELLO, more

"The Seraph" from *35MM*, based on a photograph by Matthew Murphy
    Genre: Ballad, Folk Song, Gay Interest
    Key/Range: F major; C3 to A4
    Context: *A sinful man finds hope when he is discovered by one who spurs him toward goodness.*
    Watch This Performance: http://www.youtube.com/watch?v=FbA4dbkfa9s *(performed by Jay Armstrong Johnson)*
    Suggested Audition Cut: "I don't believe in God" to the end.
    Band Parts Available: GUITAR, more

"Stupid Boys"
    Genre: Comedic, Jazz Ballad, Gay Interest
    Key/Range: E major; C♯3 to F♯4
    Context: *While anxiously anticipating a love interest's call, a man proclaims that boys are stupid; however when he realizes his "Special Someone" isn't going call, he recognizes that he, in fact, is the stupid one.*
    Watch This Performance: http://www.youtube.com/watch?v=ZcESBIBcmDQ *(performed by Matt Burrow, Colleen Hazlett-O'Brien, and Alex Keiper)*
    Suggested Audition Cut: "Oh, he loved me Sunday" to the end.
    Band Parts Available: PIANO, GUITAR, BASS, DRUMS, CELLO, SYNTH, more

"To Do"
    Genre: Love Ballad
    Key/Range: D major; A3 to D5
    Context: *After a series of unrequited loves, a hopeful romantic vows to move forward.*
    Watch This Performance: http://www.youtube.com/watch?v=qaFqlj1_dF4 *(performed by Natalie Weiss)*
    Suggested Audition Cut: "All the time that I've waited, wasting time" to the end.
    Band Parts Available: PIANO, GUITAR, BASS, DRUMS, more

"The View From Here" from *DARLING*, book by B. T. Ryback
    Genre: Ballad
    Key/Range: D♭ major; D♭4 to A♭5
    Context: *16-year-old Ursula Morgan sits on her windowsill, reflecting on her neglected childhood and hopeful for a better future.*
    Watch This Performance: http://www.youtube.com/watch?v=EkVj6yNXdWc *(performed by Grace Wall)*
    Suggested Audition Cut: "Ursula Morgan, here at the sill" to "Out of view from here."
    Band Parts Available: PIANO, BASS, DRUMS, CELLO, SYNTH, more

"What It's Worth" from *OUT OF MY HEAD*
    Genre: Ballad
    Key/Range: A♭ major; C3 to G4
    Context: *A man proclaims that when you love someone, you sometimes need to go through the painful process of letting them go.*
    Watch This Performance: http://www.youtube.com/watch?v=LlUsRptZPWo *(performed by Jeremiah Downes, Matt Burrow, Colleen Hazlett-O'Brien, Sarah Gliko, Alex Keiper, and Michael Phillipe O'Brien)*
    Suggested Audition Cut: "This is not the end" to "When you love someone you let them go."
    Band Parts Available: PIANO, BASS, DRUMS, more

"When Lily Came" from *DARLING*, book by B. T. Ryback
    Genre: Sexy Story Song, Lesbian Rock
    Key/Range: E♭ minor; G♯3 to F5
    Context: *Ursula tells an elaborate lie about Lily, a burlesque dancer, whom she claims has kidnapped her and forced her to dance in her club.*
    Watch This Performance: http://www.youtube.com/watch?v=QpQxJeC9lR4 *(performed by Jenny Powers, Grace Wall, Catherine Brookman, Jennifer DeRosa, and Katie Gassert)*
    Suggested Audition Cut: "Round Lily came near a dozen girls" to end, or from the key change to F minor to the end.
    Band Parts Available: PIANO, GUITAR, BASS, DRUMS, CELLO, SYNTH, more